HUMAN ANATOMY MADE EASY

CHILDREN'S SCIENCE & NATURE

BABY PROFESSOR

EDUCATION KIDS

Have you ever wondered what our body consists of?

Do you wonder how we move, how we breathe, how we eat and how we get rid of our waste?

The way our bodies
work is impressive. The
human body is the most
amazing system on
Earth.

ACTIVITY
HEALTHY HEART
IMMUNE SYSTEM
HY DIET
BALANCED MIND

MY BODY

eyebrow
eye
nose
mouth
chin
chest
arm
hand
leg
toe
forehead
ear
cheek
tooth
tongue
lip
stomach
knee
foot
neck
finger
ankle

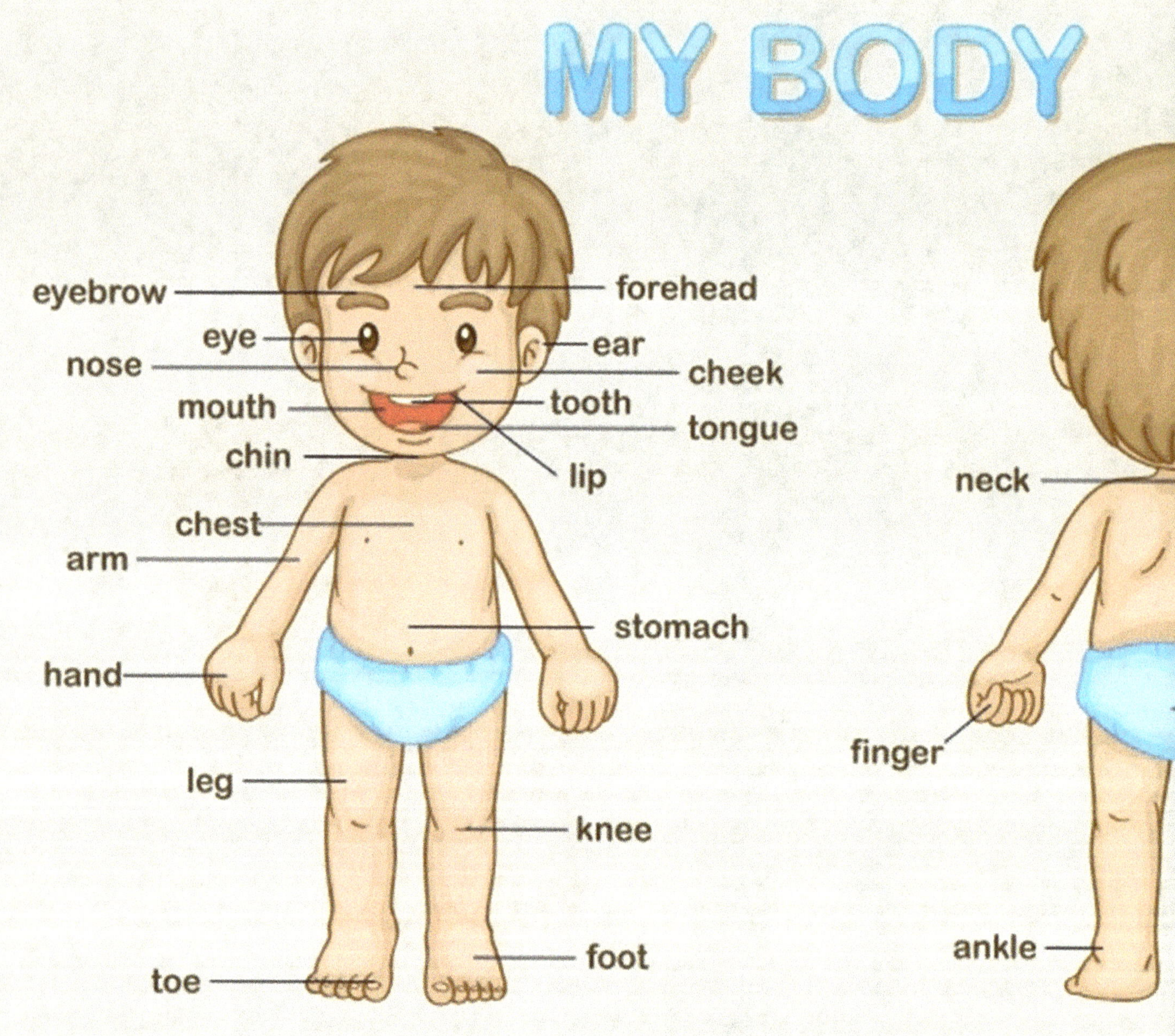

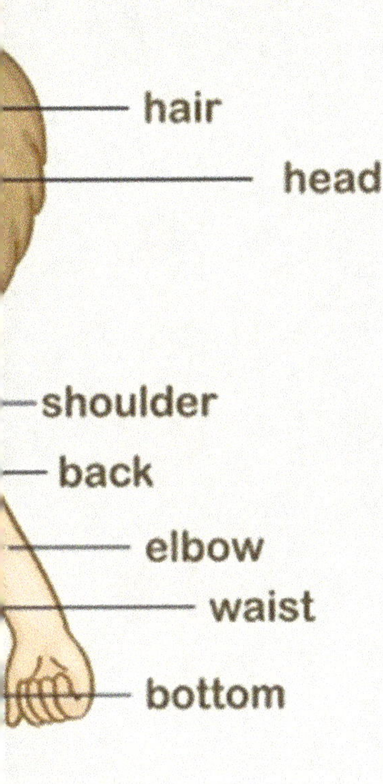

Read on and learn about the structure of your body and how the parts work together.

See what's inside you.
These are the parts of
our body that help us
keep on living.

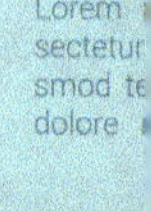
Hear
Lorem
sectetur
smod te
dolore

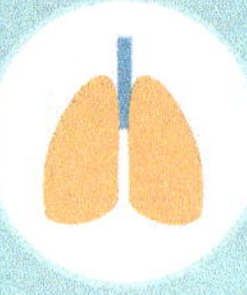
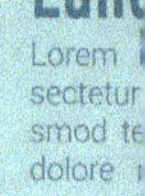
Lung
Lorem
sectetur
smod te
dolore

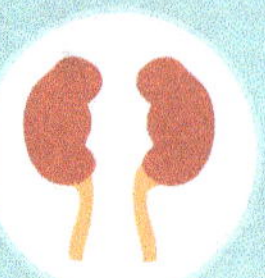
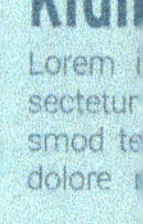
Kidn
Lorem i
sectetur
smod te
dolore

Blac
Lorem
sectetu
smod te
dolore

Bon
Lorem i
sectetur
smod te
dolore

BODY

GRAPHICS

Brain

Lorem ipsum dolor sit amet, consectetur adipiscing elit, sed do eiusmod tempor incididunt ut labore et dolore magna aliqua. Ut enim ad

Stomach

Lorem ipsum dolor sit amet, consectetur adipiscing elit, sed do eiusmod tempor incididunt ut labore et dolore magna aliqua. Ut enim ad

Liver

Lorem ipsum dolor sit amet, consectetur adipiscing elit, sed do eiusmod tempor incididunt ut labore et dolore magna aliqua. Ut enim ad

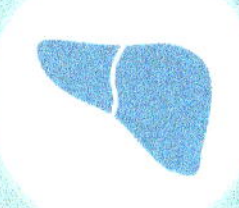

Small intestine

Lorem ipsum dolor sit amet, consectetur adipiscing elit, sed do eiusmod tempor incididunt ut labore et dolore magna aliqua. Ut enim ad

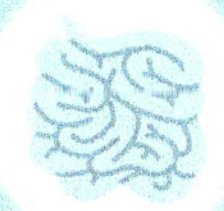

Large intestine

Lorem ipsum dolor sit amet, consectetur adipiscing elit, sed do eiusmod tempor incididunt ut labore et dolore magna aliqua. Ut enim ad

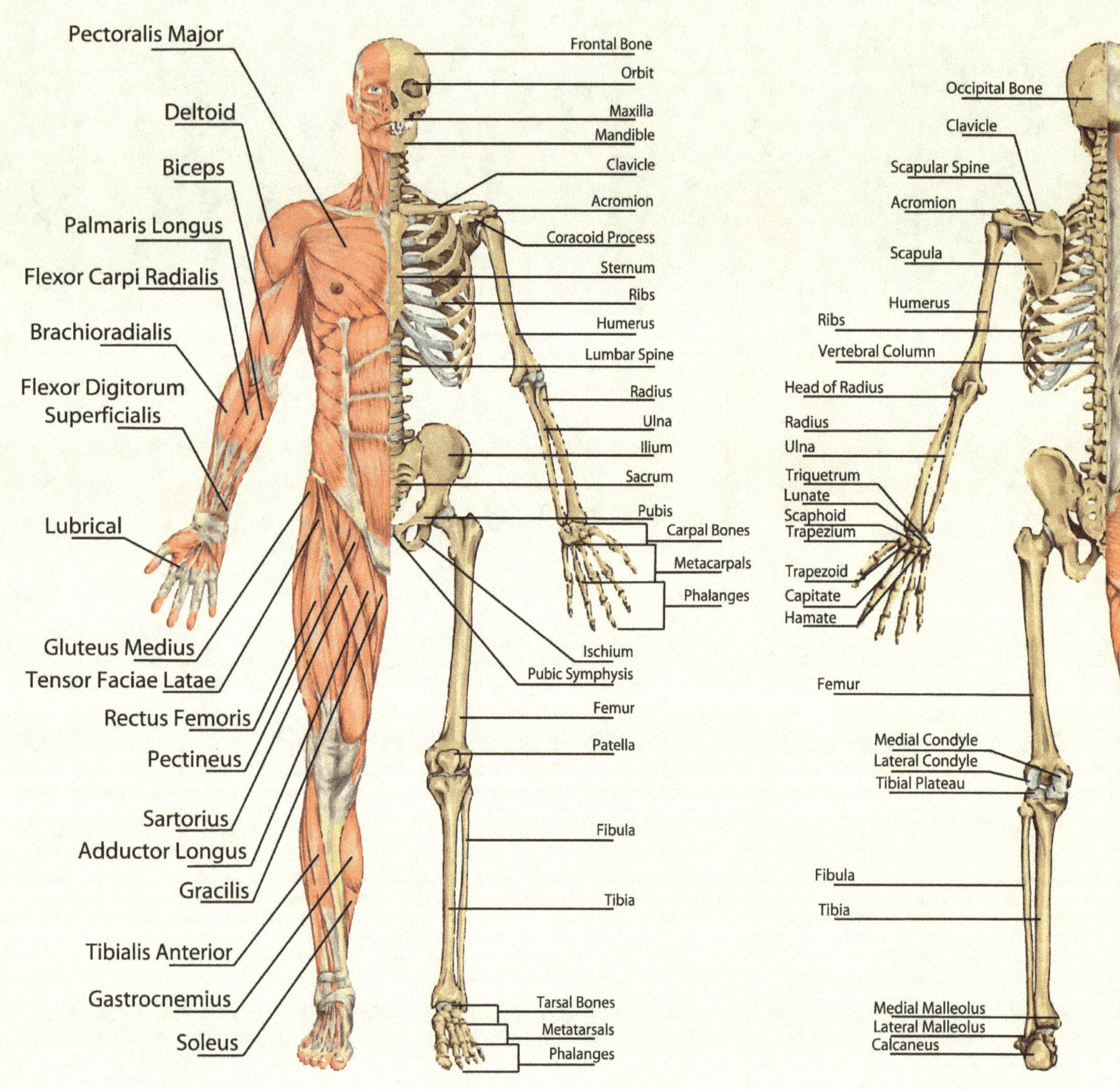

Pectoralis Major
Deltoid
Biceps
Palmaris Longus
Flexor Carpi Radialis
Brachioradialis
Flexor Digitorum Superficialis
Lubrical
Gluteus Medius
Tensor Faciae Latae
Rectus Femoris
Pectineus
Sartorius
Adductor Longus
Gracilis
Tibialis Anterior
Gastrocnemius
Soleus
Frontal Bone
Orbit
Maxilla
Mandible
Clavicle
Acromion
Coracoid Process
Sternum
Ribs
Humerus
Lumbar Spine
Radius
Ulna
Ilium
Sacrum
Pubis
Carpal Bones
Metacarpals
Phalanges
Ischium
Pubic Symphysis
Femur
Patella
Fibula
Tibia
Tarsal Bones
Metatarsals
Phalanges
Occipital Bone
Clavicle
Scapular Spine
Acromion
Scapula
Humerus
Ribs
Vertebral Column
Head of Radius
Radius
Ulna
Triquetrum
Lunate
Scaphoid
Trapezium
Trapezoid
Capitate
Hamate
Femur
Medial Condyle
Lateral Condyle
Tibial Plateau
Fibula
Tibia
Medial Malleolus
Lateral Malleolus
Calcaneus

What is human anatomy?

It is the scientific study of the way the parts of the human body interact and function as a unit. Anatomy explores the structures of the human body.

Skeletal System

It is composed of all the bones and the joints in the body. The skeletal system acts as the body's support.

Human Skeletal System

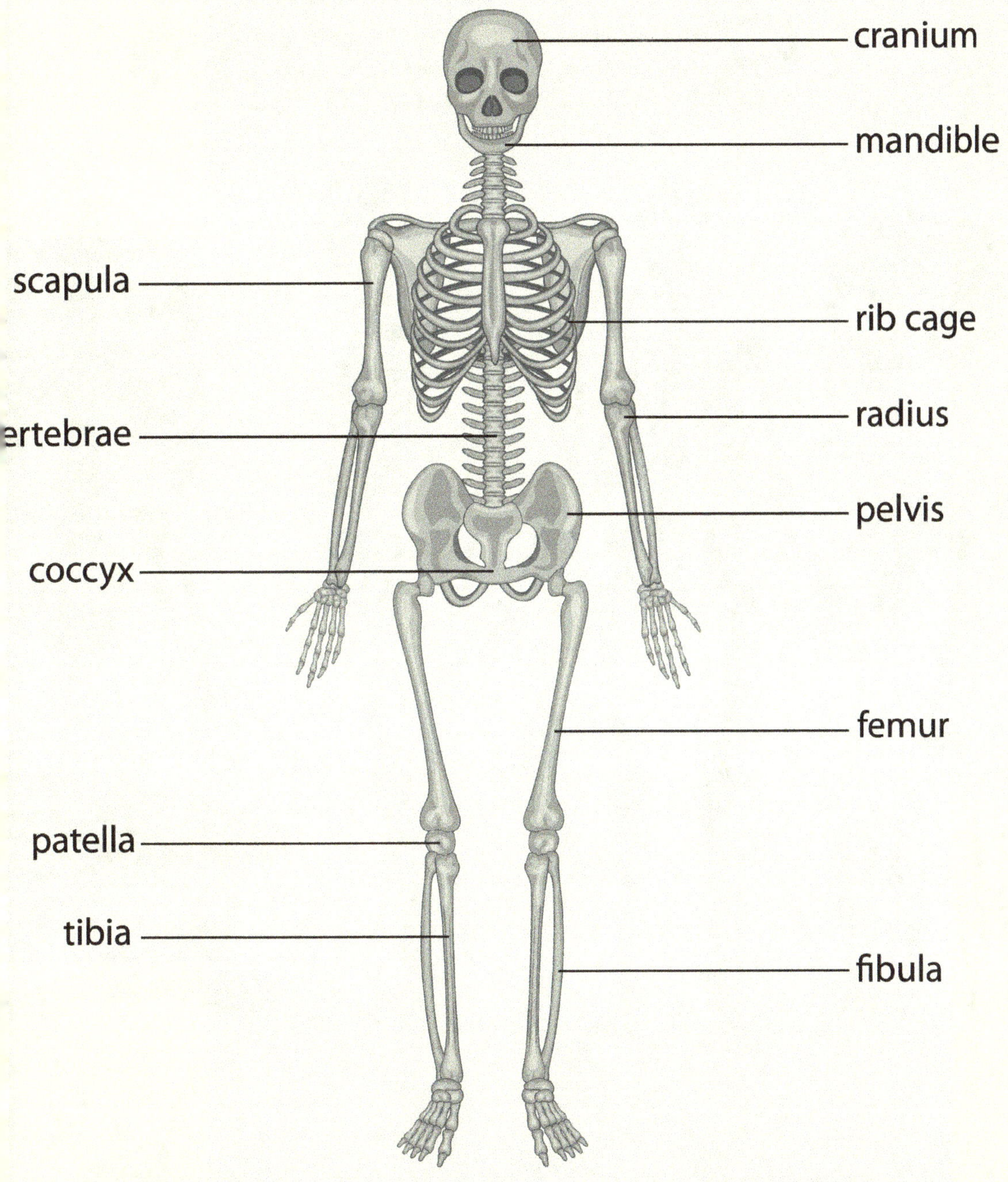

SKELETON

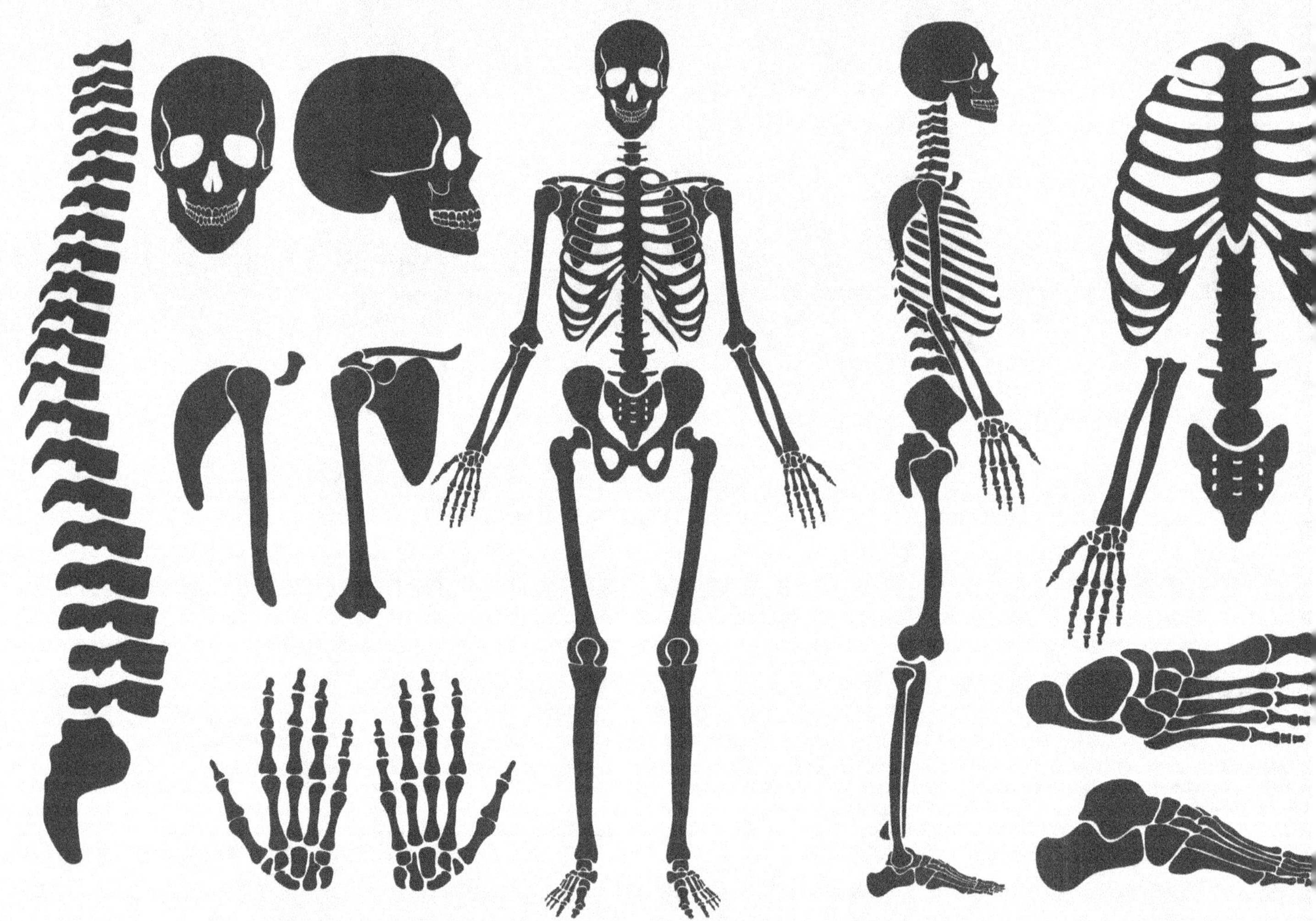

Moreover, the skeleton protects the soft tissues in the body. The bones are made up of cells, protein fibers and minerals.

Cardiovascular System

The heart is the central organ of the cardiovascular system. Other components are the blood vessels.

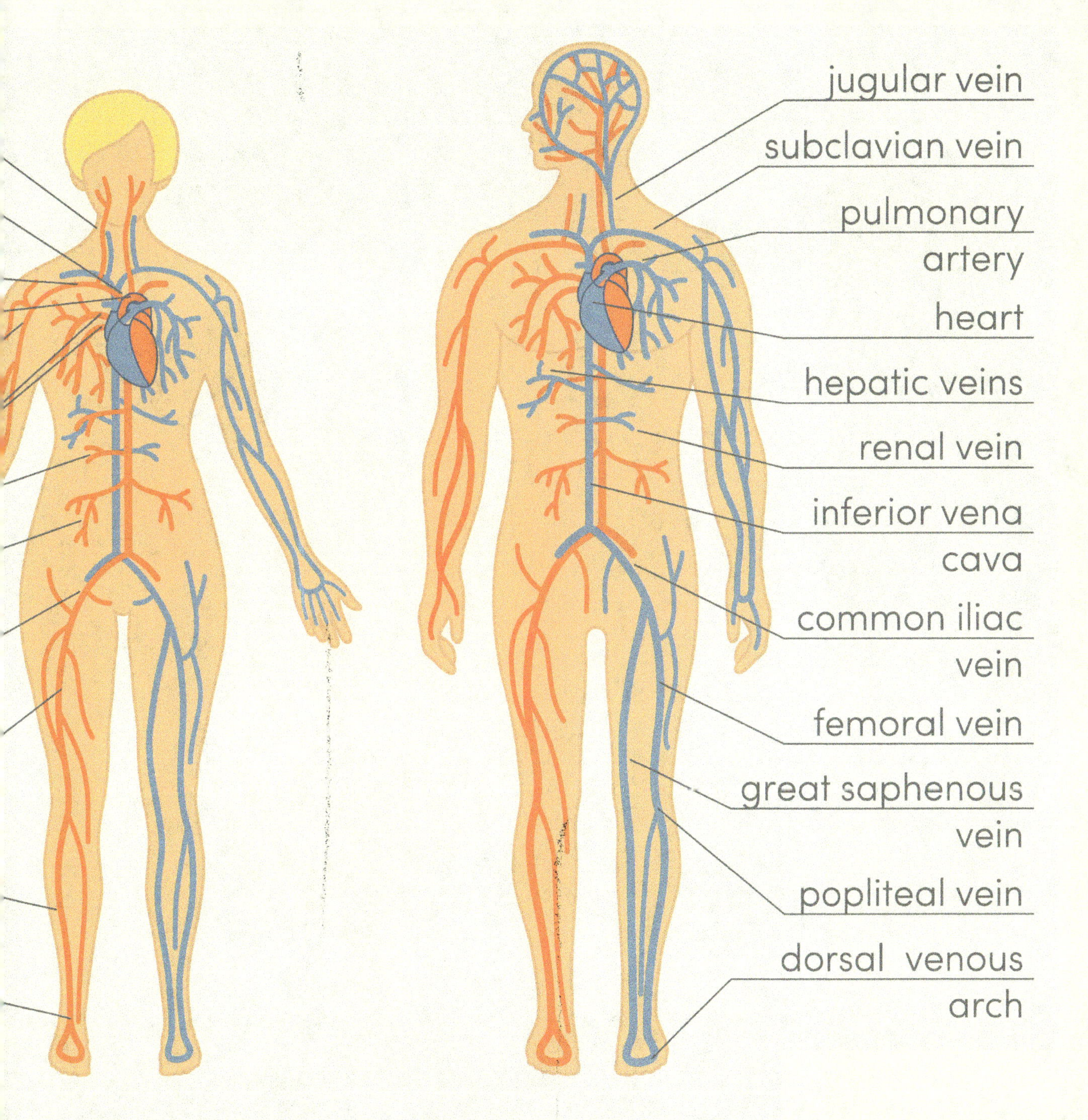

jugular vein
subclavian vein
pulmonary artery
heart
hepatic veins
renal vein
inferior vena cava
common iliac vein
femoral vein
great saphenous vein
popliteal vein
dorsal venous arch

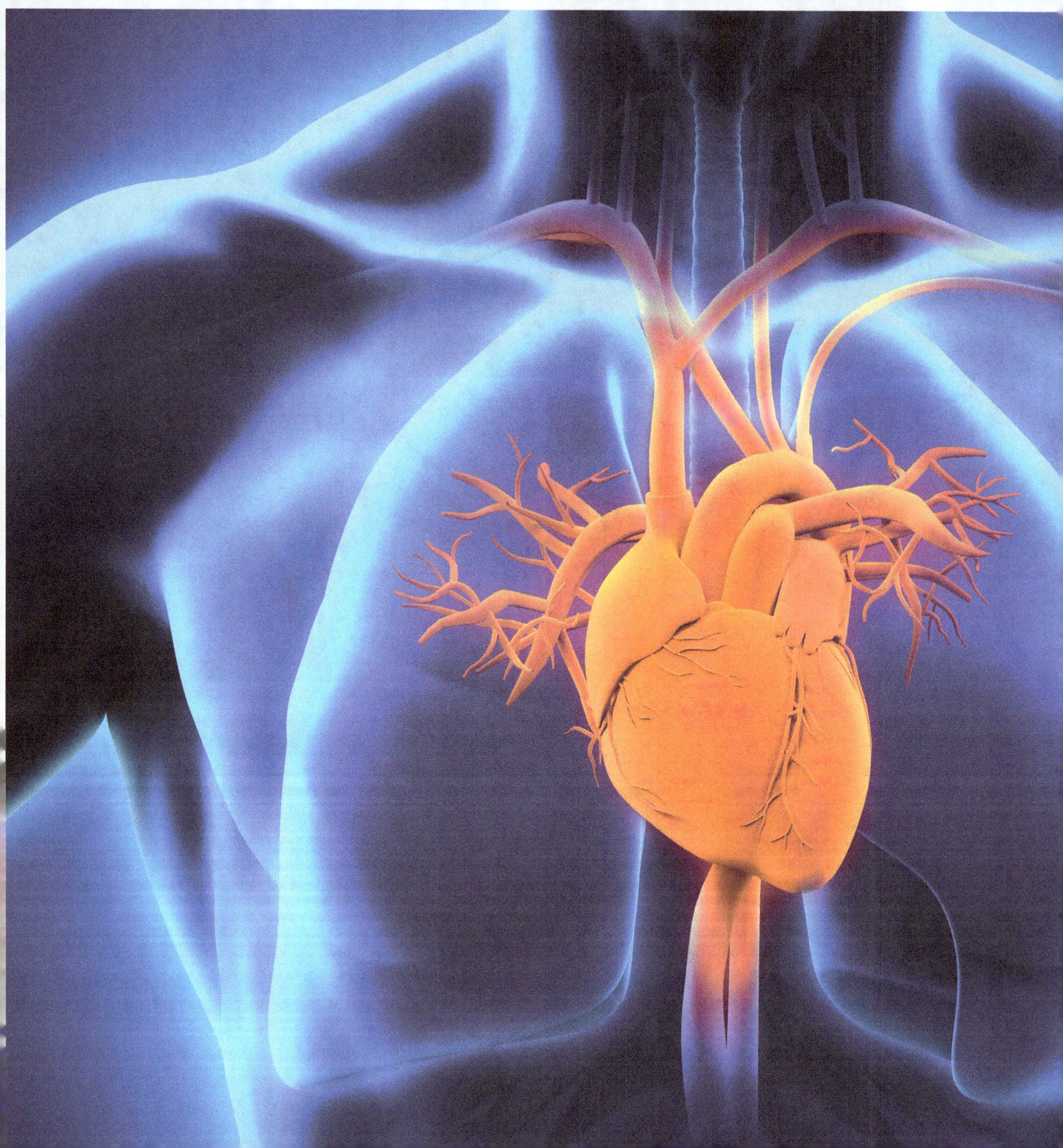

The **cardiovascular system** uses the blood stream to deliver oxygen, hormones, and nutrients to all parts of the body and to take away cellular wastes.

Muscular System

Muscles make the human body move. There are roughly 700 named muscles attached to the skeletal system that contribute to almost half of a person's weight.

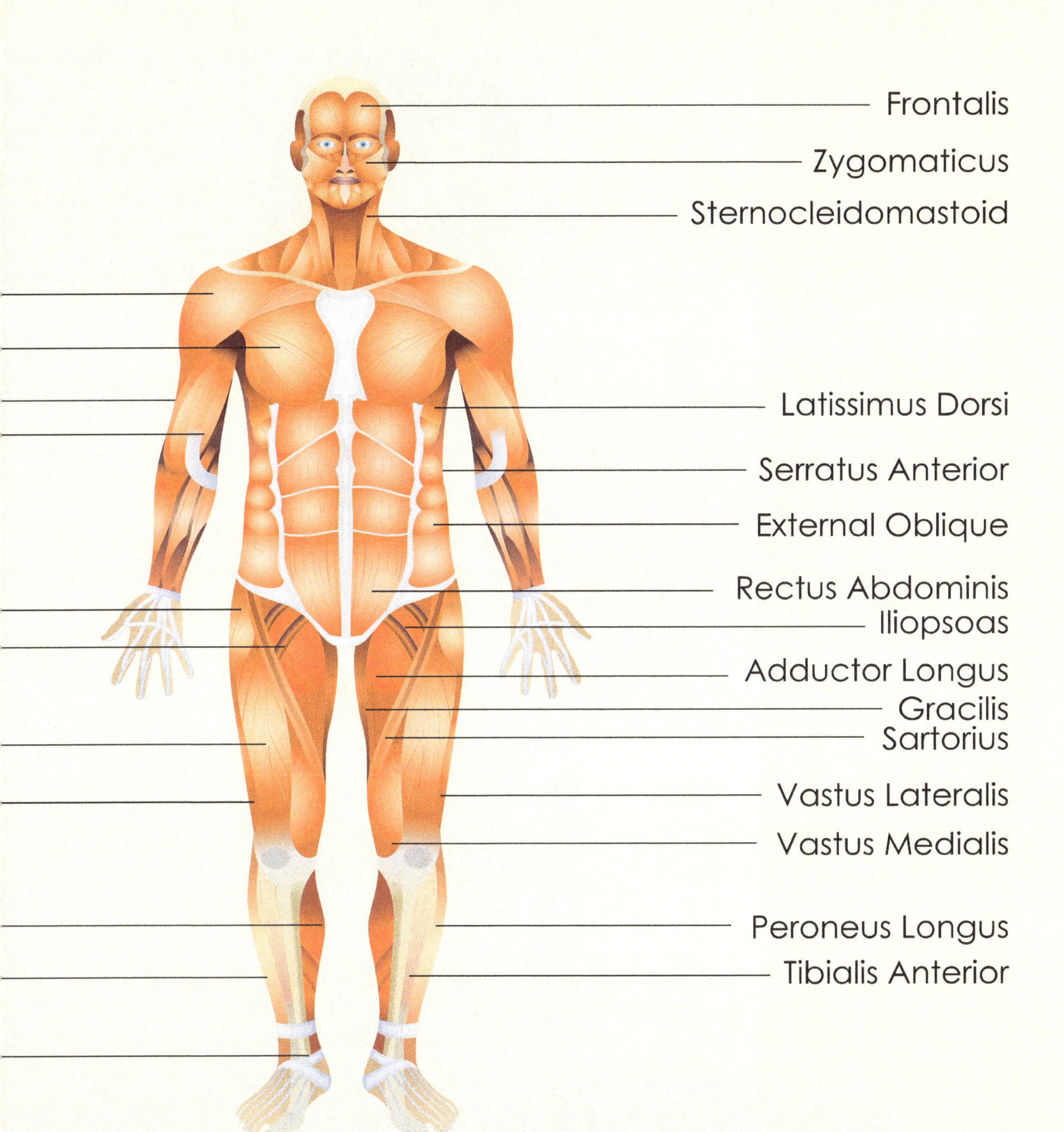

Frontalis
Zygomaticus
Sternocleidomastoid
Latissimus Dorsi
Serratus Anterior
External Oblique
Rectus Abdominis
Iliopsoas
Adductor Longus
Gracilis
Sartorius
Vastus Lateralis
Vastus Medialis
Peroneus Longus
Tibialis Anterior

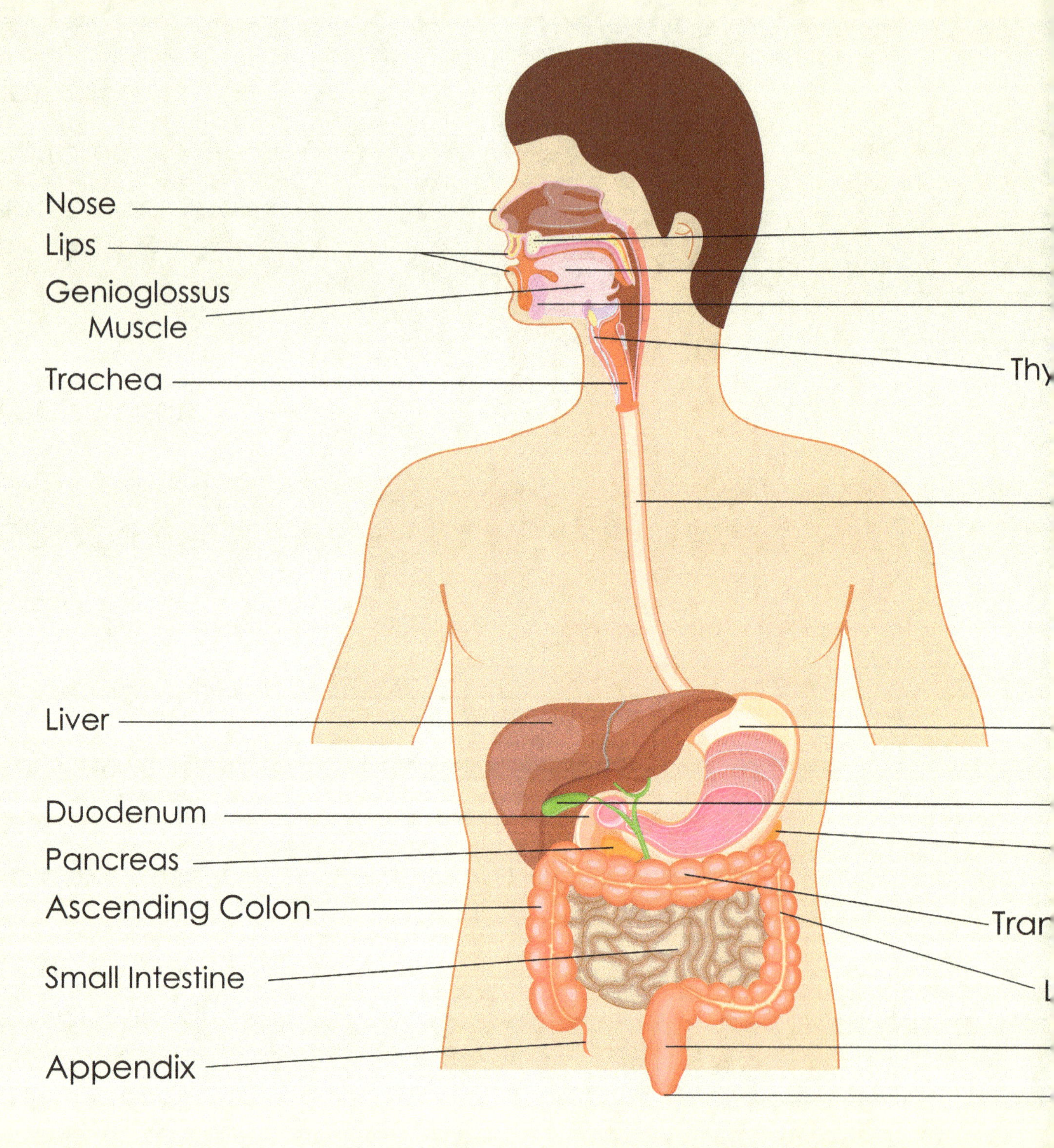

Nose
Lips
Genioglossus Muscle
Trachea
Thy
Liver
Duodenum
Pancreas
Ascending Colon
Small Intestine
Appendix
Tran

Digestive System

These are organs which convert food into energy and basic nutrients for the entire body. The major components are the mouth, esophagus, stomach, small and large intestines.

Nervous System

It is composed of the brain, spinal cord, sensory organs and the nerves. The nervous system receives information and sends signals to the whole body.

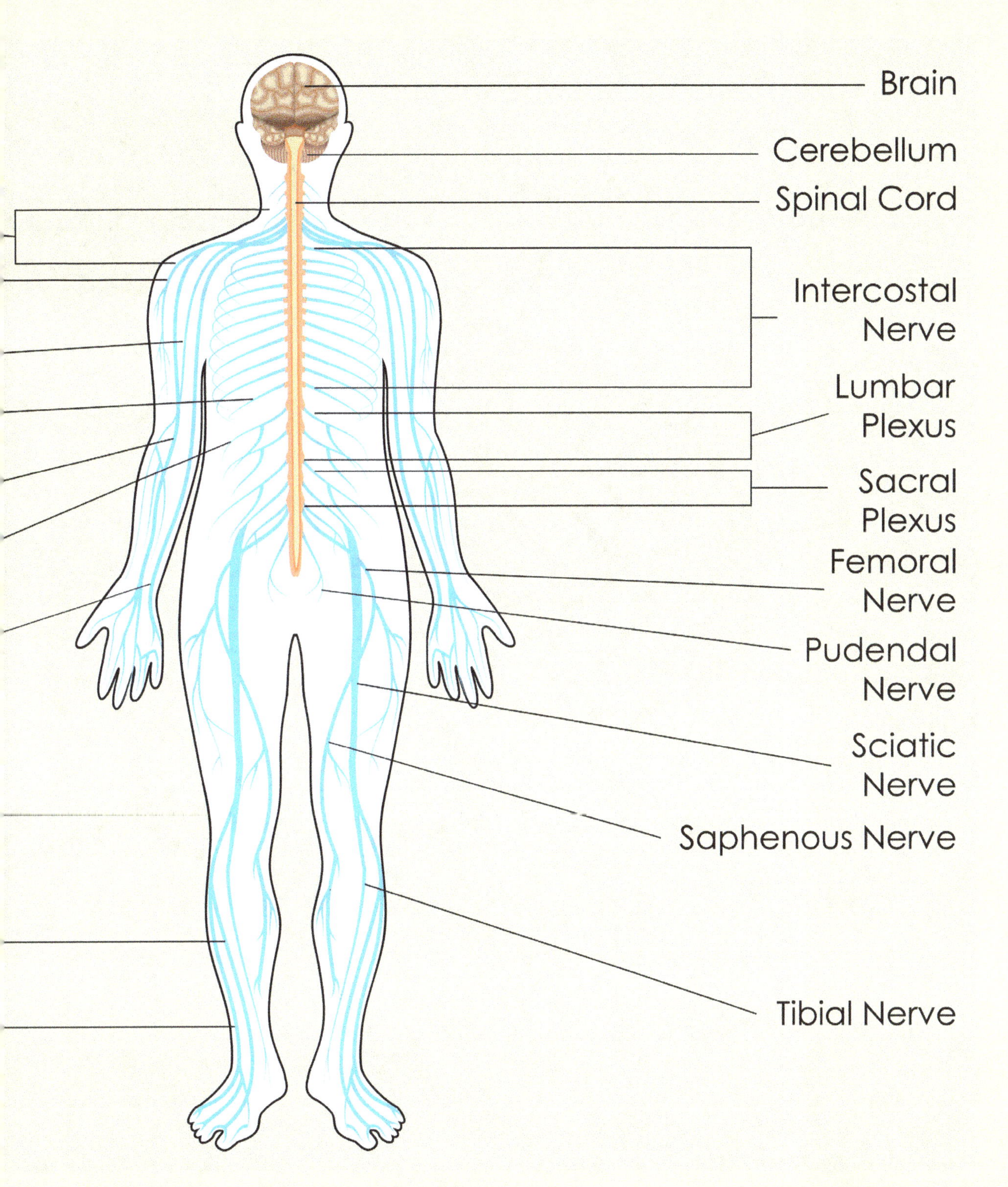

Brain
Cerebellum
Spinal Cord
Intercostal Nerve
Lumbar Plexus
Sacral Plexus
Femoral Nerve
Pudendal Nerve
Sciatic Nerve
Saphenous Nerve
Tibial Nerve

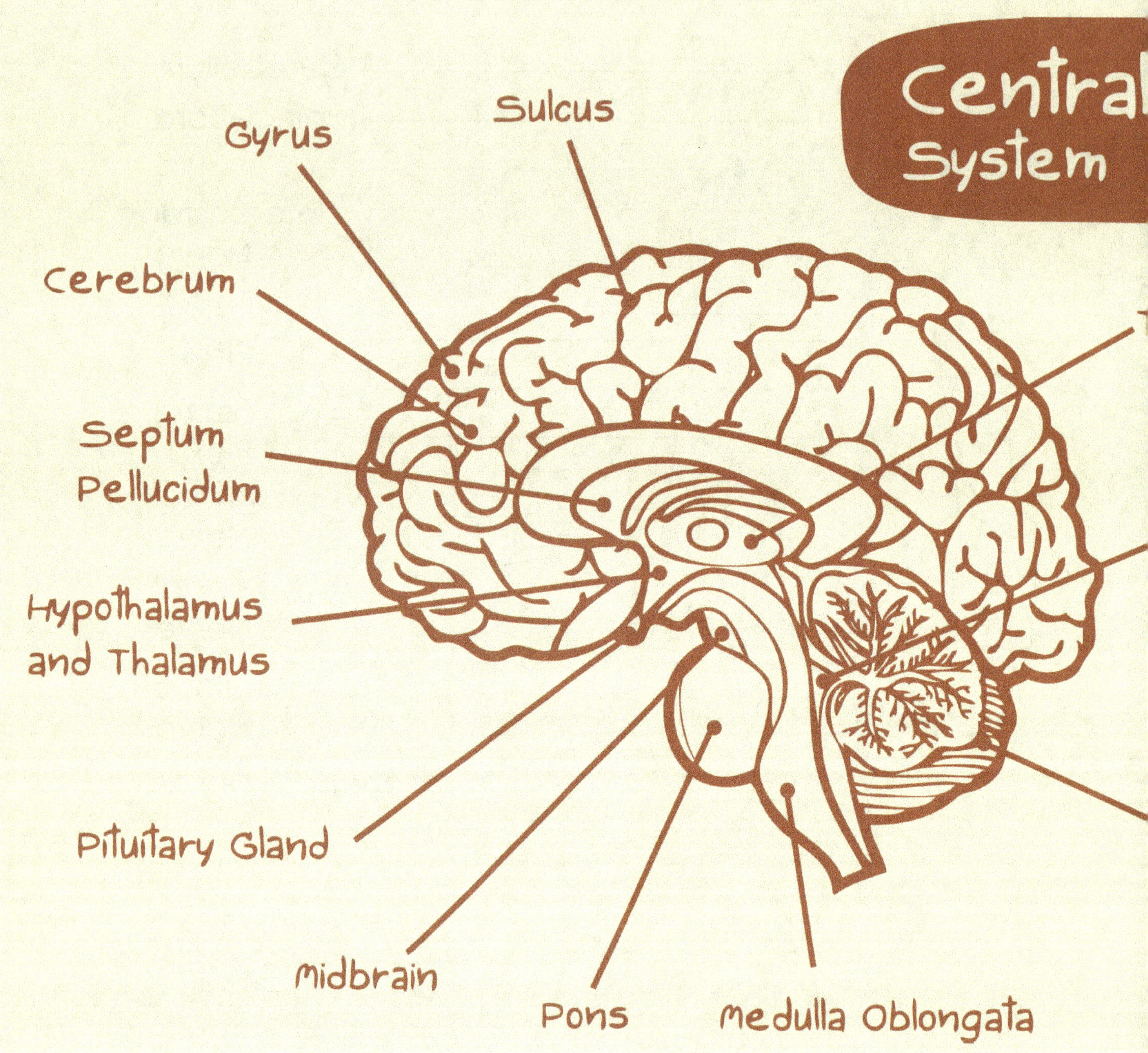
Central
System
Gyrus
Sulcus
Cerebrum
Septum
Pellucidum
Hypothalamus
and Thalamus
Pituitary Gland
Midbrain
Pons
Medulla Oblongata

The central nervous system consists of the brain and the spinal cord. It is where the decisions for the entire body are made.

Respiratory System

The respiratory system keeps us breathing. It includes the airway, the lungs and the muscles of respiration. We need oxygen in order to live.

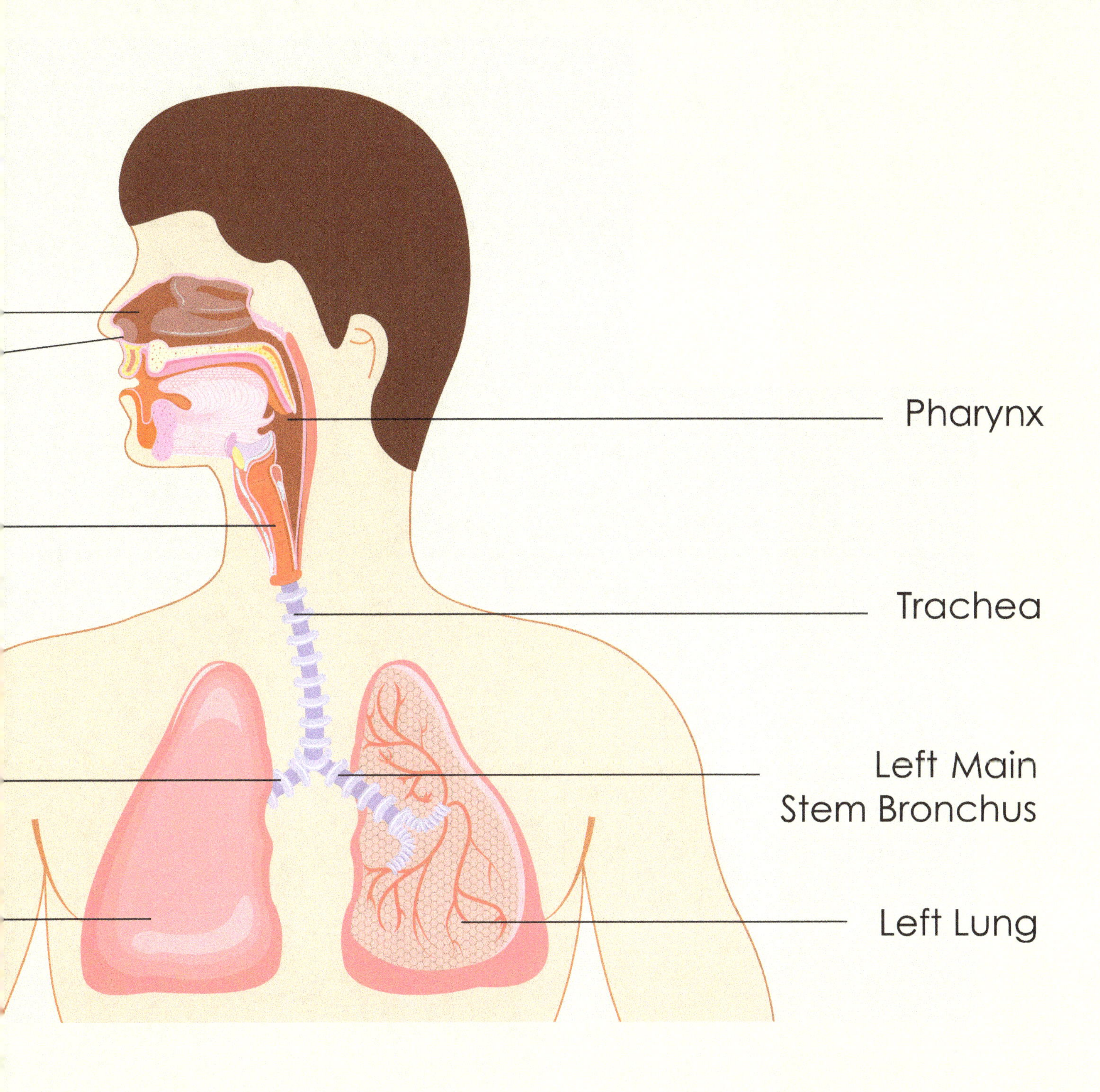

Pharynx
Trachea
Left Main
Stem Bronchus
Left Lung

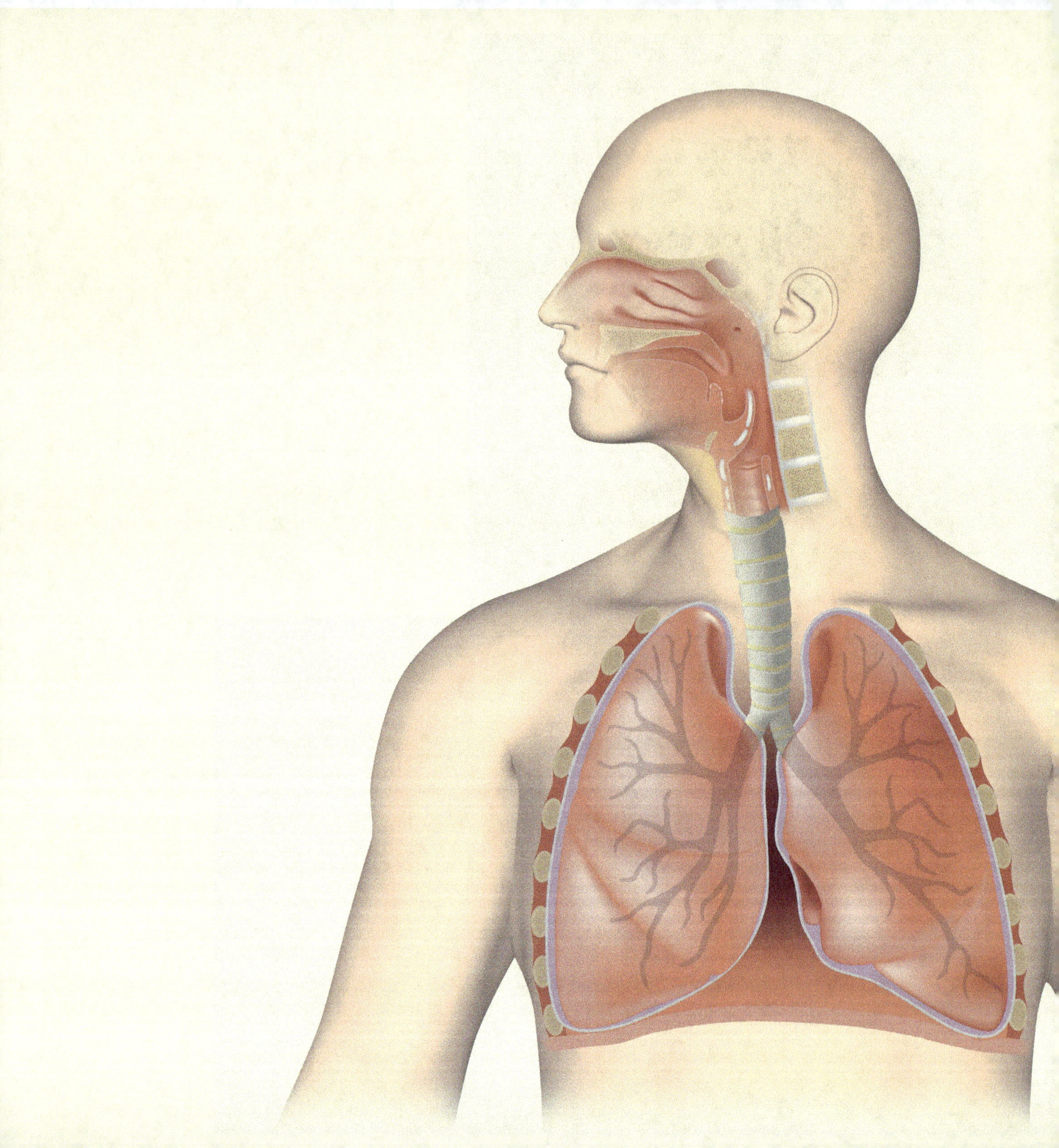

It is the responsibility of the respiratory system to give oxygen to all body cells and to remove carbon dioxide, the waste product from cells.

Urinary System

The urinary system is responsible for filtering and eliminating wastes from the body. It includes the kidneys, urinary bladder, ureters and the urethra.

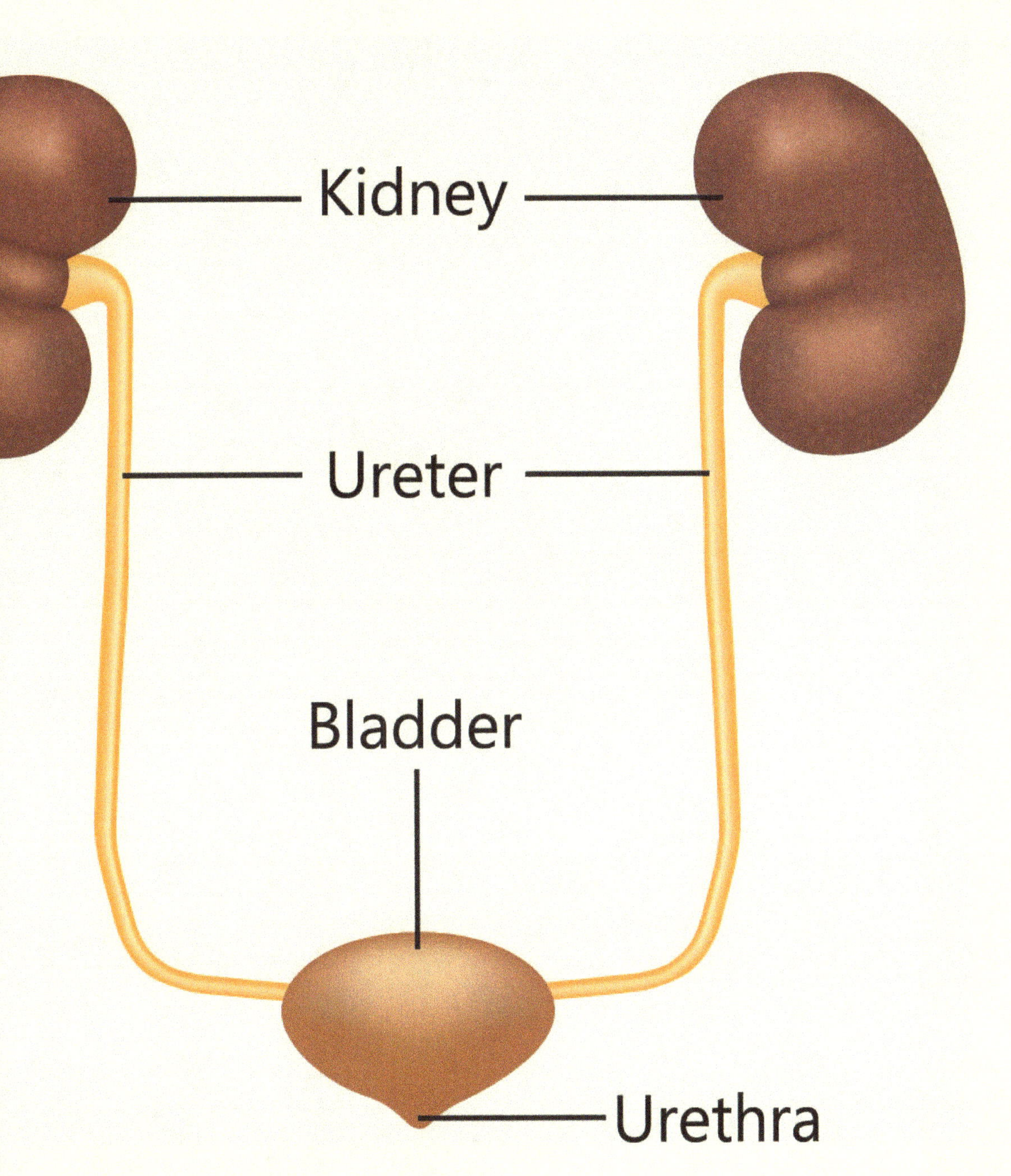

Kidney
Ureter
Bladder
Urethra

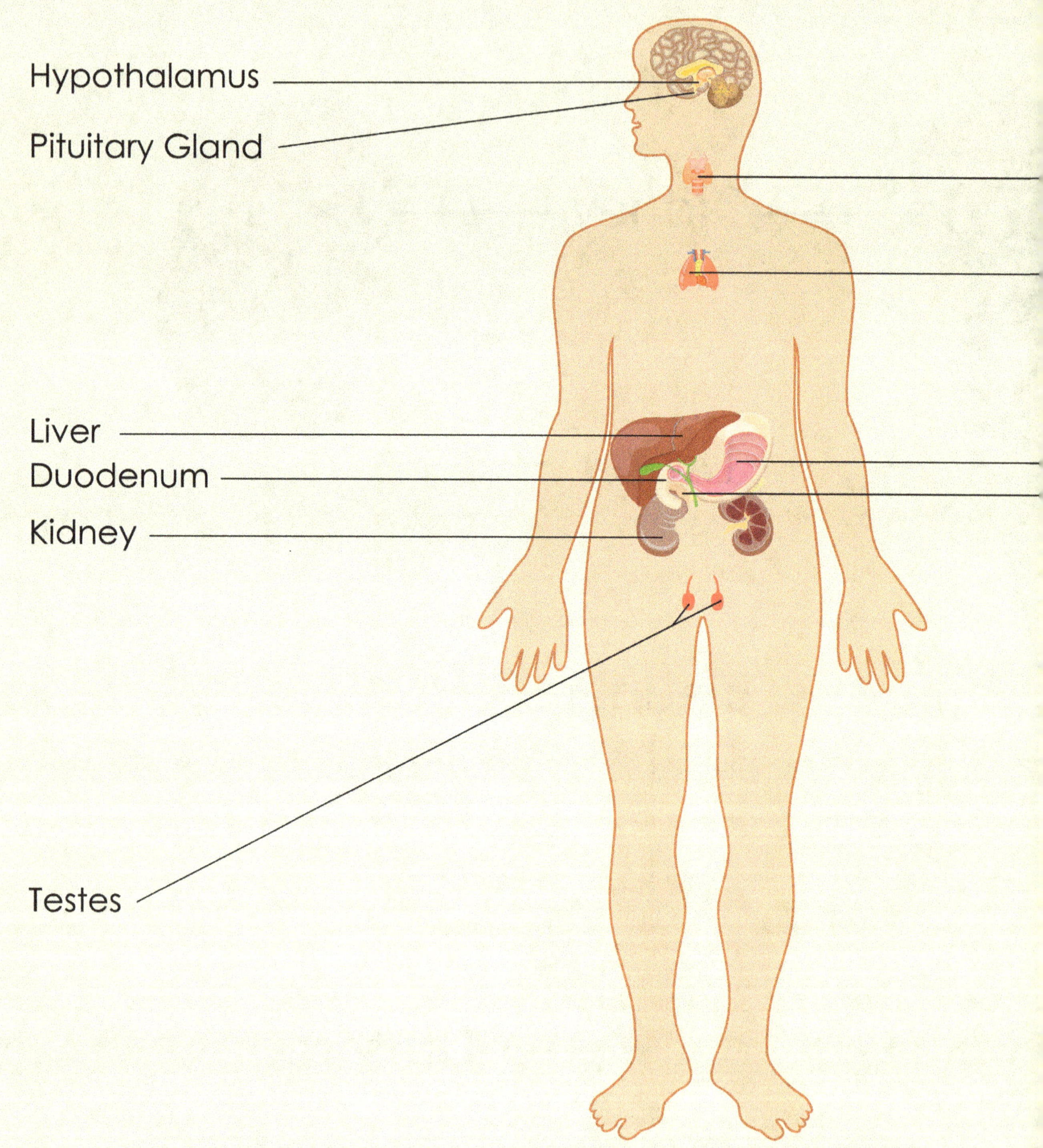

Hypothalamus
Pituitary Gland
Liver
Duodenum
Kidney
Testes

Thyroid Gland

Thymus Gland

— Stomach
Adrenal Gland

Endocrine System

It includes all the glands of the body. It also includes the hormones produced by those glands. Its main function is to keep the body's systems in balance.

The human body consists of all the structures of our physical being. It is basically composed of cells which form tissue and eventually creates organs.

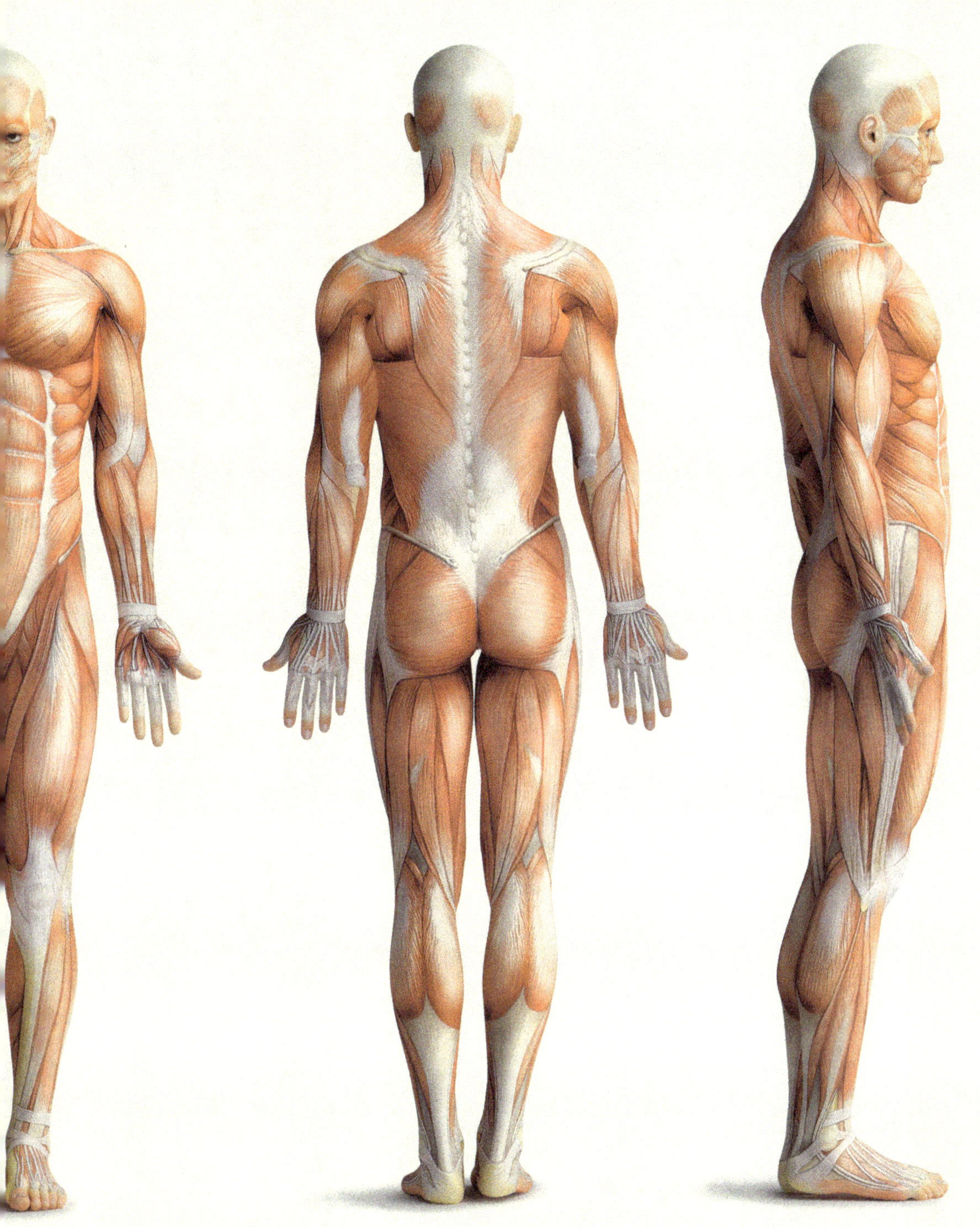

By studying human anatomy, can see how fascinating the human body is. The human body is indeed an amazing creation worthy of love and care. As we understand the human body, it gives us an idea of how we function inside.

Visit
BABY PROFESSOR
EDUCATION KIDS
www.BabyProfessorBooks.com
to download Free Baby Professor eBooks
and view our catalog of new and exciting
Children's Books

www.ingramcontent.com/pod-product-compliance
Lightning Source LLC
Chambersburg PA
CBHW081241130726
47997CB00009B/2961